Leovin B. Colibao

Bahandi

A Magnum Opus

To order additional copies of this book, contact:
Xlibris
1-888-795-4274
www.Xlibris.com
Orders@Xlibris.com

ISBN: Softcover   978-1-7960-6610-4
       EBook   978-1-7960-6611-1

Print information available on the last page

Rev. date: 10/16/2019

For God
For My Family
And For Myself

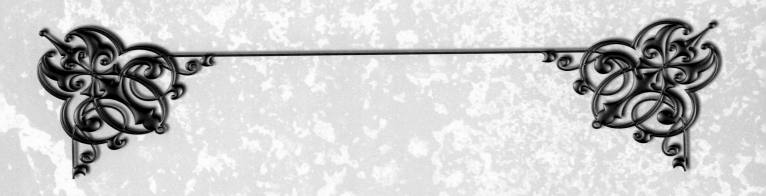

Letters of Love

Love that exudes from within, is love that is hard to find
Endures and withstands even the loudest fracas at hand
Openly accepts the imperfection of the other
Valiant, passionate, resilient, and growing together
In this world, a lot are running after the wrong person
Not realizing that someone smiles – he is the reason

But stupefied of his unrequited love, he got blind

Clouded and bounded, the other cries and is left behind
Once, the time came that the other woke up from delusion
Love that was as hot as torch is now cold and no motion
In his eyes he still see, the woman he thought he reached
But little did he know that the love that he thought he pitched
Adoration, infatuation if contemplated
One who got neglected at first, is now happy and free

Dead-end

Green leaves turn to brown
Black hair turns to gray
Eyesight will be blurry
Ev'ryone you've known have grown

Time ticks for everyone
No one is exempted
It may be alarming
But fear not and keep going

In this world of uncertainty
Where life is unpredictable
Make the best out of time
Create memories and smile

Do things that you love
Love and do them with all your heart
Friends, ladies and gentlemen
Remember me for I'll be gone

Sweetdreams

Sleep well and sleep tight
In your bed, day and night
Close your eyes and dream
There you can flee and scream

This dream of yours is your greatest aspiration
You cannot reach in reality even with big perspiration
Earn millions and be happy
Or even become Barbie

Flying cars and full of cash
Flowy gown on your birthday bash
No budget to think about
Just dream and don't doubt

End your dream by opening your eyes
But don't really say a goodbye
For tomorrow you'll hop on your bed and become unstoppable
Because in your dream you are always capable

Nowhere

I've been looking for someone
I've been looking for something
I don't know what he looks like
I don't know where to find him

I've been looking for someone
I've been looking for something
I tried as much as I could
I tried but I don't know if I should

The image is vague and unclear
The place is gloomy and unreal
I have searched in the farthest place
Not knowing I've reached the end of days

Hifalutin

You're fake, you're bogus and indeed pretentious
Living in an unreal world you created, you feel fabulous
How do you keep existing in this fake façade?
When nothing is real in your televised fraud

Feeling of satisfaction, I guess overflows you
Whenever you see people admiring your show
Emmy, Grammy and Academy Awards
Are you planning to get yourself unreal rewards?

I guess I just can't seem to understand
The feeling of fulfilment, when you are called grand
This stage where you stand seems to be so high
Since you find it hard for you to say goodbye

One day you'll wake up in the closure of your spectacle
I hope you can still live, I know it's a hard battle
The world will not be on your back for you've lost your fame
You've lost your picture in the golden frame

Under my Wings

Life is harsh
World will crash
Sky will fall
No one to call
Always remember
I am here forever

Through your darkest whiles
And the loneliest times
Just call me by my name
Or whatever you want to
Even if I am too busy
I will find a way to help you

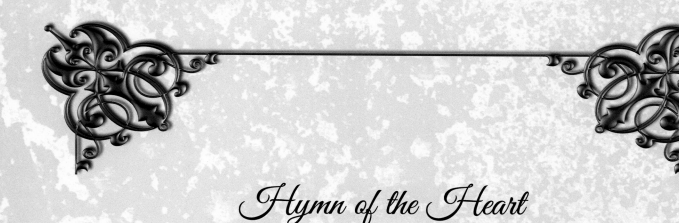

Hymn of the Heart

Listening to the song that you introduced to me
Is like going back to that time when we are walking together
Under the moonlight, you have made me see
That even the strongest wind, I can withstand and be strong

It makes me sad whenever it is played in my radio
No one knows why I still cling to that moment
In my mind it plays repeatedly like a broken video
And tears start falling because of this little memento

I hope one day when time allows we'll meet again
And you'll say hello just like yesterday
We'll listen to this old soundtrack together
And reminisce the memories that will last forever

You've changed me a lot, that I am sure
And I know this heartache could never be cured
I accepted that you will never ever be for me
But I hope you don't mind if I keep our memory

Meaningful Blues

There is this different type of sadness
Sadness that seems to be uncontainable
You don't know the reason, you don't know a solution
To ease the pain of this unexplainable internal explosion

Struggles, isolation, depression
Or merely just being different from the others
Pulls us out of the community,
where we're supposed to be

Countless nights of thinking
whether or not you should keep going
look for people who could remind you
of how important person are you

The False Jury

Brave is the soul who feels no fear
To face dropped hammer which others couldn't bear
Judge who accepts no reason but only his vision
Is neither jurist nor attended a graduation

The truth is with no degree or finished school
And tends to judge others just to sound cool
Downing others and serves as their critic
I don't think his doing anything fantastic

Yes, the sad reality of this modern courtroom
Is the existence of ignorance and unidentifiable loom
Spectators who gives sentence to trial they don't know
Hoping they'll get something, which I'm pretty sure is a no

How did we end up creating such jurists of the state?
Seeing this situation, I guess we're all going in to a bait
We're creating a future full of faultfinding ones
Is this what we end up for? Is our delicadesa gone?

You, Who is Different

You, who've been lost in dark
And for you who has no one to guide
While walking alone by your path
Let this be your light

You, who was always the laughing stock
Of even his very community
While they're happy of your sorrow
Always remember there is an uncertain tomorrow

You, who lives independently and alone
And opted to be in his comfort zone
I'll destroy the walls of your room
So that people around you see you bloom

You're not accepted of who you are
Misplaced, criticized, and insignificant mar
I am here to break these metal bars
For YOU, WHO IS DIFFERENT, to them you are at par

Happiness from Within

Hold your breath and close your eyes
See the beauty in hellos and goodbyes
The world is in chaos but you are in control
Create a world for you and your own battle

Hold your breath and close your eyes
Imagine the things you've never had
Life is unfair but you are in control
Possess the things you desire until you get bore

Hold your breath and close your eyes
Love the person you once admired
Heart can't be tamed but you are in control
Love and be loved in your own little world

Hold your breath and close your eyes
Be the person that you always wanted to be
Do it in reality for you are in control
No one can hinder you, it is your life to settle

Ageless

Come and explore the beauty
Beauty in one and everybody
Everybody exudes one
One should find it on their own

Own yourself and let no one dictate you
You decide who you are and will be
Be the person you wanted to see
See your beauty and own it

It cannot be stolen and taken
Taken for granted, it could be forgotten
Forgotten maybe but for me it will not
Not in this lifetime and the next to come

Wanderer

Finding the response to these overdue questions
Is rather exhausting instead of it to be exciting
Looking for answers from supposed to be teachers
Talking to people that doesn't even know a matter

People who are still uncertain of who they really are
Don't try to find the answers from people from a far
The answers could be found within you
It is just taking its time and waiting for the cue

It takes time to develop your identity
What you need is for you not to be blinded by society
Once you consider yourself developed
You will then be able to spread your wings from being enveloped

For those who are still looking for answer
Answer to their questions which are hard to discover
Let this be a message of advice to your wandering beauty
Don't forget that closet is for clothes and you are not something that can be folded

Refused and Unrequited

Love in its most beautiful form
is love being shared by two people.
What if you found the love of your life,
but the love you give is not reciprocated?

It may hurt you, but do you have a choice?
Are you willing to take the risk?
Some people will still hope but most of them will give up.
Will just let their feelings elapse

Unreciprocated is it worth it?
Do we deserve it?
Questions that can be answered by anyone
But only few will confront

Whatever your life's standing is
Rich or poor; ugly or beautiful
No one can be excused
In loves most unrequested form

Haikus

Rock they crumble down
To nature's great destroyers
No time for sorry

It is hot as sun
If ignored will become ice
The light will be gone

Fruits from the nature
We rarely appreciate
Now taken away

Little river flows
Countless villages use it
Yet no thanks received

Trees grow no one knows
Draws attention ones full grown
Everyone exploits

Waves crash to the shore
Bringing sands and stones with him
The shore misses them

Birds singing freely
Admired and is abducted
Freedom is stolen

Thunder and lightning
Combos sound and lighting
Beaut and destruction

Ina

Taglay mong kagandahan aking tuwinang hirang
Hindi mapapantayan ng kahit na sinuman
Napakagagarang hiyas ang iyong katumbas
Kahit hindi nakapagtapos, ika'y parang pantas

Sa lahat ng turo ikaw ay para ng guro
Punong puno ng karunungan, hindi mawawalan
Ika'y may mabuting kalooban, puro't simple
Walang kahit sinong katulad at w'lang babali

Bayani kung tutuusin at pag-iisipan
Hindi papatinag kahit na sinong kalaban
Ikaw ay mahusay sa anumang pag-alalay
Wala ng iba kundi ikaw, mahal kong Nanay

Haligi Sino Ka?

Gusali't bahay kailanman di tatayo
Kung walang aalalay dito, malamang guguho
Matayog, matikas at hindi patutumba
Gusto kong malaman, O haligi sino ka?

Itong patindig na bahagi ng ating tahanan
Nagbibigay hugis sa nakakayamot na katawan
Kung itong haligi biglang maglalaho,
Buong bahay ay tiyak magbabago

Sa bawat pangyayari, siya ay saksi
Sapagkat siya'y nariyan kahit hindi ka pa malaki
Maging sa mga panahon na di mo siya kita't dama
Inaalalayan ka niya, siya ang iyong Ama.

Sa Aking mga Kapatid

Maraming tao ang ating makakasalamuha dito sa mundo
Di mo masiguro kung sila'y mananatili o biglang maglalaho
Para sa akin, ang tunay at hindi magbabago
Ay ang pagmamahal ng ating mga kadugo't kapamilyang puro

Mga kapatid, talagang makukulit at minsan mapanakit
Hindi nagkakasundo at parating nagkakagulo
Ngunit kahit ganito pa ang parating situwasyon niyo
Sila ay nariyan para sa iyo sumaklolo

Sa aking mga kapatid, hindi man tayo palaging magkakalapit
Palagi niyong tatandaan na hindi kayo nawawaglit sa aking isipan
Kayo at ang ating mga magulang ay ang laging inaalala
Iniibig makasama sa bawat gabing natutulog mag-isa.

"

You don't deserve to sleep late night
thinking that you are not good enough.

"

Printed in the United States
By Bookmasters